CW00734565

ROMANTIC ENGLAND
THE LANDSCAPE AND ITS WRITERS

JOHN CURTIS

Text by Richard Ashby

SALMON

INTRODUCTION

So much of English literature is the literature of place. From the Brontë sisters to Jane Austen, from the Swallows and Amazons to Winnie-the-Pooh, the characters belong in the landscape with which their authors were familiar and often loved. It is impossible to associate the Brontes with anywhere other than the wild moors of West Yorkshire or Jane Austen other than with the Hampshire countryside or the elegance of Bath. Arthur Ransome first met the children in his stories when in the Lake District, and the forest around A A Milne's East Sussex home was Christopher Robin's own private world. Thomas Hardy, of course, is the prime example, so much so that much of central southern England can be defined as 'Hardy's Wessex'.

Many of the writers included here have associations with more than one place and in particular many of them lived or worked in London. Dickens, for example, is closely associated with the capital, he lived much of his life here and he worked here. It is London and the villages and suburbs of which it is comprised which is inhabited by his characters or is the object of their ambitions. Milton was a Londoner, fleeing the capital to escape the plague, Housman was a civil servant, and Wordsworth famously wrote of the view from Westminster Bridge. But it is their association with a more romantic England with which we are largely concerned in this book. While most of us live in towns and cities, it is the country of England which moves us most and it is England's poets and writers who have often captured the essence of England itself.

ROCHESTER, *Charles Dickens*
Charles Dickens spent the happiest part of his childhood in Chatham in Kent, and Rochester and its surrounding area provided the inspiration and scenes for many of his works, especially *Great Expectations*, the *Pickwick Papers* and his unfinished last novel, *The Mystery of Edwin Drood*.

HAWORTH MOOR, *The Brontë sisters*
Perhaps it is not surprising that the dramatic scenery surrounding Haworth and the intense cloistered life shared by the three Brontë sisters should have produced such powerful works of the imagination. This ruin, known as 'Top Withens', on the horizon, is believed to be the inspiration for *Wuthering Heights*.

BATH, *Jane Austen*

Although she lived most of her life in Hampshire, a county she loved, Jane Austen often visited Bath and when her father retired, the family came to live here.
The buildings of Georgian Bath epitomise the age of elegance which we associate with her novels, many of which are set here and which gently satirise its society.

MALHAM TARN, *Charles Kingsley*

When staying in the Yorkshire Dales at Tarn House, Charles Kingsley was asked about the black streaks on the face of the cliff nearby. His joking reply that a chimney-sweep must have been carried over them and into the lake gave him the inspiration for *The Water Babies* in which the abused sweep, Tom, escapes from his master and, falling into a river, is transformed.

SOMERSBY, *Alfred Lord Tennyson*

Tennyson was the Victorians' favourite poet and he was very widely read. Queen Victoria would summon him to Windsor or Osborne, made him her Poet Laureate in 1850 (succeeding Wordsworth) on the promptings of the Prince Consort, and gave him a peerage in 1883. He had come a long way from the obscure Lincolnshire rectory in Somersby in which he was born.

STOKE POGES, *Thomas Gray*

Memorising poetry as a childhood or school task is long gone, but there are a few poems, even now, still engrained in the English cultural memory. One of these is the *Elergy Written in a Country Churchyard* by the 18th century writer Thomas Gray. The poem was inspired, at least in part, by the death of his Eton school friend Richard West and, although begun earlier, was finished in 1750 in Stoke Poges in Buckinghamshire where Gray's widowed mother lived. The opening line *The curfew tolls the knell of passing day…* is one of the best known in all English poetry although few people can remember much more nowadays! The poem made Gray famous.

OXFORD, *Colin Dexter*

While the relationship between Inspector
Morse and his faithful and long suffering
assistant, Sergeant Lewis, is at the heart
of these famous detective stories, they
are firmly set in the city of Oxford.
The buildings, institutions and the people
of Oxford are an integral part of the drama.

RIVER THAMES, *Lewis Carroll*

It was in the summer of 1862 that the
Reverend Charles Dodgson and a friend
rowed the three daughters of Dean Liddell
up the Thames from Folly Bridge in Oxford
to Godstow. It was then that he began the
story that within a few years had become
Alice's Adventures in Wonderland.

SLAD, *Laurie Lee*
This was once an obscure village in an isolated Gloucestershire valley. Now millions know of it through the writing of its most famous son, Laurie Lee and his book *Cider with Rosie* in which he describes a world and way of life which has now vanished.

HARTLAND MOOR, *Thomas Hardy*
Much of Thomas Hardy's Wessex was once heathland, stretching across the southern part of Dorset as far as Dorchester. Many of his stories are set in this landscape and the hardness of their characters' lives reflects the bleak beauty of the landscape.

ULLSWATER, *William Wordsworth*

Like his successor as Poet Laureate, Tennyson, William Wordsworth had also come a long way from the reduced circumstances and the radical politics which made him an early supporter of the French Revolution. By the end of his life he had become financially and socially very successful and a political reactionary. His poetry and other writings did much to instill a love of the Lake District into the English people although he hated the beginnings of the mass tourism that his writings encouraged. He and his sister Dorothy were great walkers, tramping all over the area. His poem *To Daffodils*, inspired by a walk on the shores of Ullswater, is still voted the country's favourite.

EXMOOR, *R D Blackmore*

Lorna Doone by R D Blackmore is still read today. It is a story of high passion and clan rivalry, set in the 17th century on Exmoor in North Somerset. Blackmore knew the area well. His grandfather had been Rector of the little village church at Oare in which the heroine, Lorna, is shot during her wedding.

WHITBY, *Bram Stoker*

Bram Stoker took many holidays in Whitby and he wrote *Dracula*, his classic horror story here. During a great storm a ship arrives at Whitby on the Yorkshire coast, the only remaining crew member, the dead captain, lashed to the mast. As the ship runs aground a great black dog leaps ashore and disappears into the darkness. There is a great sense of foreboding in the narrative.

CONISTON WATER, *Arthur Ransome*

Generations of young people have followed with pleasure and envy the exploits of the *Swallows and Amazons* in the Lake District. Arthur Ransome, who loved the area and lived here for much of his life, took features from both Windermere and Coniston Water to make his lake. Peel Island became 'Wild Cat Island' where the Swallows make their first camp.

THE POTTERIES, *Arnold Bennett*

The novels of Arnold Bennett are now rather out of fashion. He was born in Hanley, one of the 'five towns' which make up modern-day Stoke-on-Trent. It is the industrial landscape, here captured at the Gladstone Pottery Museum, which frames his stories of those who live and work in the 'Potteries'.

HILL TOP, *Beatrix Potter*

Beatrix Potter was a lonely London child who loved the family holidays in the Lake District, and later made this area her home. Her early books, especially *The Tale of Peter Rabbit*, were so successful that she was able to buy this farm at Near Sawrey, recognisably the setting for some of her later stories.

SALISBURY, *Anthony Trollope*
The very name 'Close' conjures up a self-contained and inward looking world of intrigue, petty jealousies and rivalries along with intense friendships and great intimacy. It was in Salisbury that Trollope had the idea for *The Warden*, the first of the *Barchester Chronicles*.

LYME REGIS, *John Fowles*
As well as the setting for much of Jane Austen's *Persuasion*, Lyme Regis is at the centre of John Fowles' 1969 semi-historical novel, *The French Lieutenant's Woman*. The 1981 film has the iconic image of a cloaked Meryl Streep gazing out over the grey sea from the Cobb.

RYE, *Henry James and E F Benson*
18th century Lamb House, now in the care
of the National Trust, has major literary
associations. Henry James, the American
author who lived much of his life in England,
bought this house in 1898 and lived here
until his death. E F Benson succeeded him
and set his popular novels about Mapp and
Lucia in this picturesque little town.

SELBORNE, *Gilbert White*
After some years in Oxford, Gilbert White
returned to his birthplace in Hampshire to
become its curate. He spent much of his
time observing the natural world around
him and recording it in letters to friends
and in a diary. His friends persuaded him
to publish his observations in *The Natural
History and Antiquities of Selborne*, for
which he is still remembered.

MOORGREEN RESERVOIR, *D H Lawrence*
D H Lawrence, the son of a Nottinghamshire miner, used many local scenes around his home village of Eastwood, near Nottingham, in his novels. A real drowning in this reservoir, then much deeper, is reflected in a similar accident in *Women in Love*. The reservoir also appears as 'Nethermere' in both *Sons and Lovers* and *The White Peacock*.

ASHDOWN FOREST, *A A Milne*
Generations have been brought up on the *Winnie-the-Pooh* stories and the poems of A A Milne. For children and those still children at heart, they have an abiding appeal. The stories have been translated into many languages, including Latin and have been searched for deep psychological meaning but they are still best read at bed-time, just before falling asleep. Many of the sites which form part of the stories can be identified in this part of Ashdown Forest, near Hartfield, in Sussex, including 'Hundred Acre Wood', the 'Six Pine Trees' and this bridge. Christopher Robin and his friends played 'Poohsticks' here, dropping their twigs into the river on one side and rushing across to see which came out from under the bridge first.

MAPLEDURHAM HOUSE,
Kenneth Grahame

Kenneth Grahame began his famous *The Wind in the Willows* as a bed-time story for his son, Alistair. It was never intended for publication and when finally published in 1908 (illustrated by E H Shepard who also illustrated the 'Pooh' books) it made little initial impact. Nevertheless, over the years the story of the adventures of Rat, Mole, Badger and their friends, including the irresistible Mr Toad (modelled on the badly behaved Alistair himself) has become a great favourite. Many of the scenes are based along the River Thames between Pangbourne and Henley and Mapledurham House is one of the models for 'Toad Hall'.

DARTMOOR, *Sir Arthur Conan Doyle*

The famous Sherlock Holmes story *The Hound of the Baskervilles* was inspired by a tale of a great black dog told to its author, Sir Arthur Conan Doyle, by a local man while out walking on the moor. Hound Tor is a natural rock formation but local legend claims that it is a dog turned to stone by witches.

BATEMAN'S, *Rudyard Kipling*
Born in India and widely travelled, Kipling lived at Bateman's in Burwash, Sussex from 1902 until his death in 1936. He is remembered and often condemned as the 'Poet of Empire', but some of his best works for children were written in this house and 'Pook's Hill' can be seen from its windows.

THE NEW FOREST, *Captain Marryat*
Frederick Marryat retired from his position as a Captain in the Royal Navy in 1830 in order to write. In his time he was best known for his sea stories but his most enduring story, which still appeals today, is *The Children of the New Forest*, set in the English Civil War.

HELFORD RIVER,
Daphne du Maurier

An inlet on this beautiful estuary has been immortalised by the writer Daphne du Maurier in her romantic novel *Frenchman's Creek*. She first came to Cornwall as a child for her parents had a holiday home near Fowey. She fell in love with the area and lived here much of her life, finding it the only place where she could write. Many of her novels are set here. A deserted house nearby, 'Menabilly', was the inspiration for her novel *Rebecca* with its famous opening line: *'Last night I dreamt I went to Manderley again'*. The whole area is lush with wooded creeks, sub-tropical gardens and pretty riverside villages and pubs.

CHALFONT ST GILES, *John Milton*

In 1665 the poet John Milton fled London because of the outbreak of the Great Plague and took refuge in this Buckinghamshire village in the Misbourne Valley. Here he completed his epic poem *Paradise Lost*. The 16th century house known as Milton's Cottage is a shrine to one of England's greatest poets and the garden is stocked with plants mentioned in his poems.

CHURCH STRETTON, *A E Housman*
Although born in Worcestershire, it is for his poems about *'those blue remembered hills'*
of Shropshire for which A E Housman is chiefly remembered. The poetry of *A Shropshire
Lad* idealises the English landscape and the English ploughboy but it was written in his
lodgings in suburban Highgate while working as a civil servant in London.

Published and Printed in Great Britain by
J. Salmon Ltd., Sevenoaks, Kent TN13 1BB. © 2007
Website: www.jsalmon.com. Telephone: 01732 452381. Email: enquiries@jsalmon.co.uk.

Design by John Curtis. Text and photographs © John Curtis.

All rights reserved. No part of this book may be produced, stored in a retrieval system or transmitted in any
form or by any means without prior written permission of the publishers.
ISBN 1-84640-096-1
Title page photograph: Shandy Hall, Coxwold, *L. Sterne*. Half title page photograph: London.
Front cover photograph: Rydal Water, *W. Wordsworth*. Back cover photograph: Stratford-upon-Avon, *W. Shakespeare*.